£3.95

BRISTOL ON OLD POSTCARDS

Compiled by
Janet and Derek Fisher
Mildred and Francis Ford
(Founder members of Bristol Postcard Club)

TRAMWAY CENTRE & HARBOUR, BRISTOL.

**Published 1983
by Reflections of a Bygone Age,
Keyworth, Nottingham.**

Reprinted 1985 and 1987

**Printed by Edwin Packer & Johnson Ltd.,
Dakeyne Street,
Nottingham.**

Acknowledgements :
The compilers would like to thank Jan Bishop for the loan of postcard no. 183,
and Mr and Mrs. Daffurn for their help with information on card no. 84. They
hope that all these postcard dealers who have supplied them with cards will
continue to do so!

ISBN 0 946245 06 1

INDEX

INTRODUCTION

Picture Postcards were not introduced in Britain until 1894, though they had been popular on the Continent for over 20 years. The early British cards were known as Court Cards (size 115 x 89 mm), smaller than the Continental size of 140 x 89 mm, and the message had to be written on the same side as the picture, leaving the back for the stamp and address. This obviously inhibited the possibilities for illustrations, so when the Post Office permitted the use of the larger-size card (1899) and the 'divided back' (1902) where message and address occupied the same side, the publishers were able to exploit the postcard much more effectively, and a flood of cards on every imaginable subject was produced.

The postcard fulfilled several functions : it was a medium for communicating simple messages and greetings (mail was reliably delivered within 24 hours, and, over short distances, on the same day). Firms used them as advertising material and correspondence cards. Photographs of special events and disasters provided a unique pictorial record of local happenings. Comic postcards gave people the opportunity to send risqué messages to their friends. Soon, the collecting of all these cards became a major hobby, and the reign of Edward VII paralleled the 'golden age' of Picture Postcards, with many thousands of families amassing vast numbers sent from all over Britain (and, for those with wealthy connections, the Continent). Specialist magazines catered for the craze, and publishers produced cards on all kinds of themes : railways, actresses, military, shipping, glamour, children, heraldic, royalty, political — as well as greetings, comic cards and street scenes. The Great War saw new themes developed — patriotic, political satire, and beautiful silk cards, embroidered in France, and sent home by British tommies to be lovingly treasured. Postcard collecting ceased to have the same meaning and appeal after the war, though. The quality of production deteriorated (some of the best pre-1914 cards had been printed in Germany), the postage rate doubled, and the national mood and social conditions had changed out of all recognition : it was a new era, with changed values and priorities. 'Golden Age' postcards lay neglected in their albums in attics for years, until a few enthusiasts in the 1950's ushered in a new-found appreciation for the beautiful old cards to a whole new generation. Their availability, though, remained confined to the shelves of occasional book and antique shops, and new-wave collectors didn't find it easy to build up collections. All that changed in the 1970's. A travelling exhibition organised by the Victoria and Albert Museum, the emergence of specialist dealers, magazines, catalogues and fairs, had the effect of encouraging a host of new collectors and a consequent upsurge in prices. By then, Edwardian albums were emerging from the attics, as their original owners or their sons and daughters died. Now, the hobby is thriving, and the beautiful postcard issues of the Edwardian era are once again lovingly collected.

The cards chosen for this book represent only a fraction of those available featuring Bristol and its environs, but hopefully they will give readers a flavour of life in the Edwardian city — and of the riches waiting an old picture postcards.

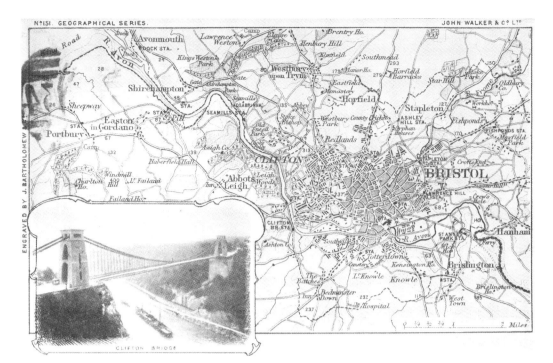

1. This map shows Bristol, and surrounding area, in the first decade of this century. Postally used 1903 at Clifton. Picture includes vignette of Suspension Bridge. Published by John Walker and Co. No. 151 in their 'Geographical' series. Message reads : *"Very wet this morning, but fine and windy this afternoon"*.

BRISTOL.

2. Coat of Arms. This shows the castle which was damaged in the Civil War and demolished by the local people who used the stone for other buildings. The ship shows that Bristol is a port, (at one time the second most important in the country). The Scales of Justice show that Bristol was an Assize city. The crest and supporters were granted by Elizabeth I. Postcard published by C.W. Faulkner.

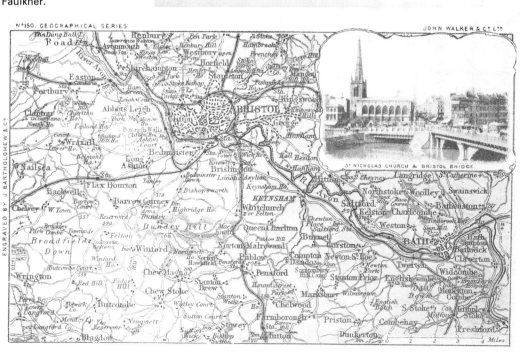

3. Map showing Bristol, Bath and surrounding villages, with vignette of St. Nicholas church, which is part of the old city wall. Postally used 1912. Same series as first card, published by John Walker and engraved by J. Bartholomew and Co.

3

4. Wine Street, c. 1904. Photographed from the site of the Civic High Cross. Pleasance and Harper are now in Clare Street; most of the buildings in this part of the city were lost in the Blitz of 1940-1941. Card by Valentine's of Dundee.

5. High Street, postally used 1911. Taken from Bristol Bridge, with the corner of St. Nicholas church just visible on the left. The Scholastic Trading Co. can be seen in its prominent corner site to right of picture. Christchurch tower and spire are rising majestically in the background. Card published by Burgess and Co. of Bristol in the 'Bee' series.

6. Old Dutch House, postally used 1910. This was situated on the corner of High Street and Wine Street. Legend has it that this house was brought over from Holland in the 17th century, hence the name. The policeman is standing approximately on the site of the High Cross. Only the building on the right stands now in its original state. An extremely popular picture postcard view.

4

7. Castle Street, c. 1925. Photograph taken looking toward Peter Street. Some of the household names have survived in the rebuilt shopping area of Broadmead. A lively photograph, with costers, cyclists, and people strolling in the sunshine. The car on the right was the registration number CJ 817. A superb postcard by local photographer Garratt.

8. Castle Green, c. 1895. Little Peter Street runs off to the right. The "Cat and Wheel" was rebuilt in 1900 and was one of the old buildings lost in 1940, although the inn sign was saved and is now in the museum. Harvey Barton's series, posted at Bristol in November 1904.

9. Castle Street, postally used 1906. Another busy scene : note the composition of the roadway — tarred wooden blocks — which remained until 1940. A Burgess and Co. production.

5

St Peters Church from Mary-le-Port St. Fred Little

10. St. Peters Church, photograph c. 1920. Mary-le-Port Street was just wide enough for one vehicle, and was a delightful thoroughfare. Dolphin Street cuts across the top, with Peter Street straight ahead. The house in the right foreground dated from the 14th century, and was pulled down in 1936. Photo by Fred Little.

11. The Post Office, Small Street, c. 1900. This street is still very much the same, with only the top floor of the Post Office missing, as it was burnt out during the war. Card postally used 1904, at Bristol. Published by Stewart and Woolf, Series 130.

12. Small Street, pre-1921. This quaint old house was demolished for the building of a bank. Notice the price of shirts : 2/6, 3/6, and 4/6. No publisher identified on the card.

The Post Office, Small Street

"A BIT OF OLD BRISTOL" SMALL ST.

A ROOM, S. PETER'S HOSPITAL, BRISTOL.

13 & 14. St. Peters Hospital. The first building on this site was at the end of the 14th century. It was rebuilt as shown in 1612 as a residential mansion. Later in its life it became a sugar house, a mint in 1695, and in 1698 a workhouse. At the time of its loss, in 1940, this very imposing building was the Registry Office. The lower card is in the "Dodson" series.

15. St. Peters church. Photograph c. 1900. The caption states, *"Bristol's Oldest Church, founded A.D. 1070"*. This church was situated within the old city wall. Only the tower and walls now remain in the Castle Park. A Fred Little postcard.

16. Mary-le-Port Street, from a photographic postcard of the late 1920's. Postally used 1937. Another view of this very interesting street, looking toward High Street. The flower market can just be seen at the far end. Published by A.G.S. and Co., Bristol.

Mary-le-Port Street, Bristol.

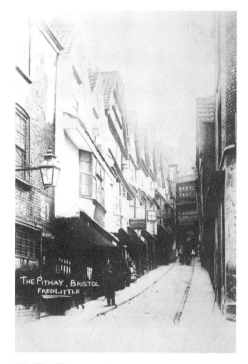

THE PITHAY, BRISTOL
FRED LITTLE

FLOWER MARKET, HIGH ST. BRISTOL

17. The Pithay, c. 1890. This quaint street was demolished in 1897 for Fry's Chocolate factory. Postcard published by Fred Little.

18. Flower Market. One piece of old Bristol, built in 1745, which happily survived the air-raids. Through the archway can be seen the beginning of Mary-le-Port street. It's still a hive of activity and wonderful smells. Card postally used at Clifton in October 1908.

Corn St Bristol

AGS & Co 433.

Broad St Bristol.

AGS & Co 434.

19. Corn Street, c. 1914, postally used 1918. Miraculously, this remains intact, the only change being in the building occupied by Thomas Cook, which is now a bank. All Saints church can be seen in the centre, and the Corn Exchange to the right of it, with the "nails" outside. Lovely open top car, registration number Y1712, is parked on the right. Postcard by A.G.S. and Co. no. 433.

20. Broad Street, c. 1920's. St. John's church and arch are in the centre of picture, the only surviving gate to the original walled city. The Guildhall on the left is early Victorian, being opened in 1846 on the site of a much earlier building, where Judge Jeffries held his "Bloody Assize" in 1685. Another A.G.S. production, no. 434, in the 'Chatterton' series.

21. Quarter Jacks and Dutch House, postally used 1920. Christchurch with St. Ewen, built in its present form in 1790. The quarter jacks were taken from an older building facing Wine Street, prior to that date, and erected in their present position in 1913. They are still a great attraction to visitors and Bristolians alike. The figures in the foreground seem to be selling flags; for the war wounded, maybe? Postcard published by Viner and Co., Bath.

Quarter Jacks & Dutch House, BRISTOL. 779

22. Clare Street and Baldwin Street, pre-1920. A busy scene in the centre of Bristol, with tram no. 38 travelling from Ashley Down to the Centre. The double pillar box, centre foreground, was removed a few years ago. Posted in London in November 1922.

23. St. Stephens church, from a photograph of the late 1920's. The tower of this city church was rebuilt in the 1470's, and the city parish extends out into the Bristol Channel. A postcard by Boots of Nottingham in their 'Pelham' series.

24. Stock Exchange, St. Nicholas Street. Postally used 1924. A beautiful building, recently renovated, showing carvings in their full glory.

25. Wesley's Statue. John Wesley came to Bristol in 1739, and held his first meeting in a field at Rose Green. The New Room was the centre of Methodism in the West Country, and Wesley lived there for many years. Postcard no. 32 by Garratt.

26. Broadmead, early 1920's. The Odeon cinema now stands on the site occupied by Fry's factory, (note the horse waiting to be harnessed into wagon in archway). The Greyhound Hotel, at the far end on right of picture, is the only original building left in this area. Coloured postcard by Max Ettlinger and Co. Ltd., series 1096.

27. Union Street and Horsefair, 1915. Wonderful Temperance Parade where now stands John Lewis and other multiple stores. This card shows the 1915 Lord's Day Union procession on May 29th.

28. Christmas Steps. Originally a steep and dangerous short cut from the bank of the river Frome. At the top of the steps there is an inscription recording — *"This street was steppered, done and finished September 1669"*. Card by Valentine's, posted at Fishponds in April 1917.

29. St. James church and park, postally used 1904. Monastery church of the Benedictine order, and finished about 1160, it became the church of a new parish in 1374. Undivided back postcard published by Stengel and Co.

30. Horsefair, postally used 1907. The St. James fair was held here, and plague victims were buried. The remains were exhumed and re-interred in Avon View cemetery, when the site was used for the first of the post-war stores. Postcard by national publishers Hartmann.

31. North Street, c. 1920. 11.40 a.m. on a busy day! Alas, only the Full Moon Hotel still survives. A Harvey Barton photographic postcard, no. 29.

32. Arley Chapel, situated at the junction of Cheltenham Road and Arley Hill. Designed by Foster & Wood in 1855, it is now used as a church by the Polish Community in Bristol. Posted in 1908 in Bristol.

33. Gloucester Road, postally used 1917. The cab shelter on the left dates from the 1880's, and is now demolished. The building near the tram was Bristol Tramway garage, and later became Morgan's department store, then Colmers, and now Homeplan. Card by Harvey Barton.

GROSVENOR ROAD. BRISTOL. 2.

ASHLEY DOWN RD. 33.

34. Grosvenor Road, Bristol, 2. Postally used 1923. The Children are intent on "watching the birdie!" The shops on the right have been demolished and the ground landscaped. This Garratt postcard illustrates perfectly the appeal of these superb local and social history documents for collectors.

35. Ashley Down Road. Taken in the mid-twenties. Note the dancing bear on the right, a rare sight in British streets. Photographic card by anonymous publisher.

ASHLEY DOWN BRISTOL. 266.

36. Ashley Down pre-1920. Two Midland trains near Ashley Hill station. The large building on the skyline is the orphanage set up by George Müller in 1870, now used by Bristol Polytechnic.

37. The Baptist Chapel and Gloucester Road, Horfield. This began life as a mission at Rowlay Road, (now no. 10 Thornleigh Road), on Easter Sunday 1882. Seven years later, an "Iron Chapel" was erected on a plot of land in Gloucester Road. In 1895 a school chapel was built in Brynland Avenue to accommodate 500 people. Because of its phenomenal growth, the erection of the present building, with frontage on Gloucester Road, to accommodate 1100 people, was dedicated on 16th January, 1901. Anonymous publisher.

38. Horfield Barracks, c. 1910. The Barracks were built in 1847, but have since been demolished and replaced by offices, although the chapel survives. Interesting motor-bike with basket side-car on the right of picture. Postally used in 1912.

39. Filton Tram Terminus, postally used 1921. Tram no. 44 came into service in 1900, and was broken up in 1939. A.G.S. and Co. postcard.

13

BRISTOL, TRAMWAY CENTRE.

40. Tramway Centre, c. 1906. The frontages of the Central and Derrick's restaurants were altered to match the Tramways offices, with clock, and these buildings are now undergoing further restoration. Derrick's restaurant is advertising Fry's and Cadbury's chocolate. As yet there is no Hippodrome : this was to come in 1912. Postcard by Raphael Tuck and Sons in their 'Town and City' series 2011 — Bristol.

The Tramways Centre, Bristol.

41. Tramway Centre, postally used 1914. The tram in the foreground is travelling on the Brislington-Hotwells route. An interesting feature is the man on the right winding a lamp globe into its socket. Postcard by Harvey Barton and Son.

St Augustines Parade, Bristol.

42. St. Augustines Parade, postally used 1907. In the foreground is the Dublin shed, where the Irish boats unloaded. This is the area of water now covered by the centre gardens. A pleasure boat can also be seen.

43. Rupert Street and Quay Street, c. 1920's. The building on the right belonged to J.S. Fry, chocolate manufacturers, and the auctioneers were Geo. Nichols Hunt. Electricity House now stands on this site. The cast iron pillar under "Auction Rooms", is the access to the river Frome, which flows under the road, and is still in use today. Postcard published by the York Publishing Co., Bristol.

44. Demerara House. A close-up of the previous picture. The figure-head came from the *S.S. Demerara* which broke her back on her maiden voyage down the river Avon in 1851. Unhappily, it disintegrated when being removed in 1931.

45. St. Mary's on the Quay, Roman Catholic church, postally used 1905. Built in 1839, the buildings on either side of the church have been demolished — the *Evening World* was published in a building at the far end of the picture until 27th January, 1962. Card in the 'Avondale series' by J.B. and S.C.

46. Baldwin Street, postally used 1916. This street came into being in 1883, and this photograph was taken facing the centre from Bristol Bridge. The elegant buildings on the right at the time of this photograph housed wine merchants and printers. In recent years it's become wholesale fruit and vegetable merchants, and now a hotch-potch of shops while still retaining the open-front wet fish shop. The New York Life building on the left corner was demolished during the war, and rebuilt in 1956. Harvey Barton publication.

47. Bristol Bridge, looking toward Victoria Street. Bristol derives its name from Brigstow, meaning "settlement by the bridge". Originally of timber, it was rebuilt in the 13th century, and the foundations were retained for the present bridge of 1768. The route of the tram is Knowle-Bristol Bridge. The lovely old building with dome was E.S.& A. Robinson, demolished to make way for Bristol's first 15 storey building, in 1962! Postcard by Burgess and Co., Bristol, and postally used in 1916.

48. Bristol Bridge, c. 1900. The oppositve view to the previous picture. St. Nicholas church in the centre has the only public clock with a second hand in England. Valentine's series.

16

Victoria Street, Bristol.

Victoria Street, Bristol.

49. Victoria Street, postally used 1910. This road was made across St. Thomas Street and Temple Street in 1871. The Reynolds Hotel on the left became Georges' Brewery offices. Young boys can be seen going about their daily business. This was a busy street in 1910, and is even more so now.

50. Victoria Street, pre-1914. Most of the buildings in the picture were destroyed during November 1940. Neptune stands in his third position! He was first erected in Temple Street, to right of picture, in 1723, moved to the end of the lane near Temple churchyard. The vicar at that time had it moved to its position in this photograph in 1872. Father Neptune was moved to the bridge head at the Centre, in 1949. W.H.S. 'Grosvenor series' postcard, no. 1084.

51. Victoria Street. Miraculously, the railway bridge and buildings survived the 1940 blitz. A statue of Queen Victoria can just be seen on the side of the George Hotel. Viner and Co. photographic postcard.

Victoria Street, Bristol.

17

52. Rest House, Victoria Street. 1914-1919. This was run by the Church of England Men's Society for servicemen during the war. Later it became a motor factors store. This building was next to Temple Colston School.

REST HOUSE. VICTORIA STREET, BRISTOL

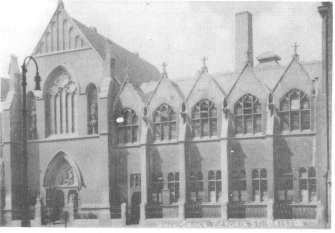

53. Holy Cross, Victoria Street. Built in 1873, this building was demolished in the 1930's when Redcliffe Way was constructed.

54. Saracen's Head Hotel. This photograph was taken about 1860, and the hotel was situated opposite Brunel's Great Western Offices at Temple Gate. One of the many pottery cones in that area can just be seen above the roof. A Fred Little card.

18

55. College Green, postally used 1919. A peaceful scene, and although it has changed somewhat in appearance, people can still sit on the grass and watch the world go by. The clock on the right has just been restored. It used to be connected to Greenwich, so that it always showed Greenwich time. All the buildings in the left background were demolished for the new Council House, and the green was lowered.

56. College Green, postally used 1918. Shows the replica of High Cross, which stood at the centre of the green. A small part of the cross can be seen in Berkeley Square. Postcard by Viner.

57. Park Street. A large number of the buildings were lost in the 1939-1945 war, but most have been re-built in similar style. Note the horses in the foreground being harnessed to the bus to assist it up the hill! A Frith's of Reigate undivided back postcard, used in April 1903. Jessica writes : *"This is the best street in Bristol"*.

19

58. The Art Gallery, postally used 1912. This was built in 1905, a gift to the city from Sir William Henry Wills, Bt. The building in the right foreground is the Blind Asylum, since removed to make way for the University. A poster on the railings advertises *"Household brushes and mats"*. Harvey Barton publication.

St. George's Church, Brandon Hill, Bristol.
Harvey Barton's Series.

59. St. George's Church, Brandon Hill, postally used 1906. Designed by Sir Robert Smirke, and opened in 1823. It was the last church to be built in Bristol in classical style. Published by Harvey Barton.

60. Christian Brothers' College, Berkeley Square. The original St. Brendan's College, which now occupies spacious grounds at Broomhill Road, Brislington. Posted in May 1906.

The Victoria Rooms

Bristol

61. Victoria Rooms, c. 1886. Built in 1839-1841, designed by Charles Dyer. Horse cabs and a cabbies' rest stand on the site, now occupied by the Boer War memorial. Stewart and Woolf postcard, series 130.

Unveiling of the Memorial to the Heroes of the Gloucestershire Regiment by Field Marshal Lord Roberts, V.C., K.G., at Bristol on March 4th, 1905. Harvey Barton Series.

62. Boer War memorial, postally used March 9th, 1905. Photograph of the unveiling of this memorial on 4th March, 1905. What service!

Royal Show 1913. His Majesty at the Victoria Rooms.

63. Victoria Rooms, 1913. The postcard shows the visit of his Majesty George V to the Royal Show, passing the Victoria Rooms en route. The statue of Edward VII and the ornamental Baroque fountain were erected in 1911. Published by Harvey Barton.

21

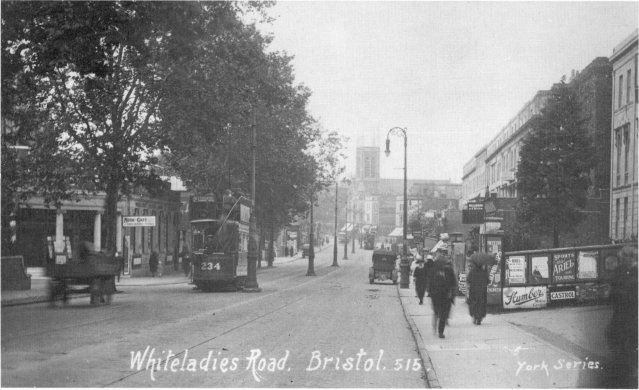

64. Alma Vale Road, postally used 1932. All Saints church tower can just be seen in the centre background. Photographic postcard by Hepworth.

65. Whiteladies Road. The tower of Tyndale Baptist church can be seen in the centre. Whiteladies Cinema on the left was opened in 1922. A lovely selection of enamel advertising plates can be seen on the wall on the right. 'York' series photographic card.

66. Whiteladies Road. Broadcasting House now occupies the building on the right. Horse-drawn transport has the freedom of the road! Posted in April 1905 at Fishponds.

67. Blackboy Inn. This building was demolished in 1874. The chapel on the right remains the same, but is now used as the Downs Fitness Centre. Fred Little photographic card.

68. Blackboy Hill, postally used 1912. Architecture is very much the same today, though trams and horse-drawn vehicles have been replaced by buses and cars! Harvey Barton and Son.

69. Royal York Crescent, Clifton. This crescent is claimed to be the longest in Europe. Building began in 1791, but was not finished until 1820. The original developer went bankrupt in 1793. Nothing changes! Empress Eugenie, wife of Napoleon III, went to school at no. 2. Postcard by Garratt.

70. Dublin Crescent, Henleaze, postally used 1930. Published by S.E. Sincock, The Library, Henleaze.

71. Henleaze Gardens, postally used 1909. Publisher was C.M. Morrish, Henleaze Road.

HENLEAZE GARDENS.

72. Victoria Road, Westbury Park, postally used 1916. Newspaper hoardings give the impression that Winston Churchill was not popular! The *Daily Mirror* advises *"Dont't wait. Go"*. The *Times* and *Mirror* also told of Allied successes in Russia, France and Serbia. Published by Viner and Co., no. 917.

Victoria Road, Westbury Park. 917.

COPYRIGHT AFS. BL. 49.   OLD MARKET STREET. BRISTOL.

73. Old Market Street, c. 1924. When pedestrians could stroll across the road, and not take their lives in their hands as they do today! A good selection of vehicles. The old Empire Theatre was demolished for the widening of Carey's Lane, now Bond Street. Postcard by A.F.S.

74. Central Hall. This was opened in April 1924, J. Arthur Rank (later Lord Rank), donating £25,000 toward its cost. So many people attended the services each Sunday, that two sittings were held at 6 p.m. and 7 p.m., 2,000 people attending each. A Garratt card, no. 726.

75. Old Market Street, pre-1924. Quite an assortment of trams and buses. The building on the right, on pillars, was noted for Pie Poudre Court, established 1483, and held every 30th September, maintaining Norman laws brought over here by the Conqueror. It was the only one of its kind in the world. A Viner photographic card.

Old Market St., Bristol. 1446.

25

76. Holy Trinity Church, St. Phillips. Designed in 1829 by Thomas Rickman and Henry Hutchinson. Now used as a centre for community relations. A "cabbies rest" is situated in front of the church. Posted at Steeple Aston in 1910.

77. Stapleton Road, c. 1914. Taken from under the railway bridge. By the tobacconist sign, very appropriate wares are advertised — *"Picture post cards — birthday cards — playing cards in great variety"*. Everyone going at a leisurely pace.

78. Tram Terminus, Stapleton Road, postally used 1930. Only the Methodist church, centre background, has disappeared; every other building remains the same.

Fishponds Road, Bristol. 99

79. Fishponds Road. This road looks the same today as in this picture. Only the tramlines are missing, and the vehicles are different! Viner postcard, no. 99.

Tram Centre, Fishponds, Bristol. 1464

80. Tram Centre, Fishponds. Virtually unchanged — only the shelter for tramways staff has been removed. Posted at Staple Hill in June 1918.

NEW STATION RD. FISHPONDS. BRISTOL.

81. New Station Road, Fishponds, postally used 1916. This road connects with the former picture, being the road where shelter stands. A Garratt publication.

82. Cross Hands, Fishponds, postally used 1923. At the junction of Downend Road and Stapleton Road, where there was then no need to worry about being breathylised! York Publishing Co. postcard.

83. Fishponds Road, postally used 1913. The only thing changed here is the removal of the tram lines. Fred Viner's publishing address is given at the back as "opposite Town Hall, Weston-super-Mare".

84. Regent Place, Fishponds. This is situated at the corner of Alexandra Park, Regent Place being the six buildings in the foreground, all part of Fishponds Road. The 'Golden Lion' was built in 1864, opened in 1866 as the 'Black Horse', with landlord Edwin Browning, wife Sarah and three sons. It became the 'Golden Lion' in 1877. In 1891, William Nash, whose family ran the 'Cross Keys', a few shops down the road, became landlord for seven years. W.B.S. postcard, posted in July 1906.

Staple Hill, High Street.

STAPLE HILL, HIGH ST.

BROAD STREET, STAPLE HILL
A7407

85-86-87. Staple Hill. The children are standing in the road with no fear for on-coming traffic, and very camera conscious! Notice the number of lamps hanging outside shops on the left. Beautiful advertisement for Downend coals in card no. 86. No publishers identified on any of these three cards.

29

ST. GEORGE

88. St. George Park. The bandstand just to the right of the picture was built in 1894, and removed in 1958. Two stacks can be seen; one behind the school (card 184) belonged to the I.C.I. works on the Netham, which was demolished in 1947, and the one on the left was for the Board Mills. Published by Shortman, Bristol, in the 'Chatterton' series.

89. St. George's Church and Fountain. The church was built in 1878, after a fire had destroyed the previous building. Sadly, it was demolished in 1976. The William Butler fountain was built on the site of the Don John Cross, the boundary of the Kingswood Forest. In the "Ozograph" series, Bristol, no. 200.

90. Avonview Cemetery, where the exhumed remains of plague victims were buried. Maybe this family have been to visit the family grave, as was the custom.

91. Bryant's Hill, St. George. This has changed very little over the years, and would be easily recognised today.

HANHAM

92. Hanham Court, postally used 1910. An earlier building on this site was given to Keynsham Abbey in about 1330, and the present house dates back to the 16th and 17th century. Posted at Hanham in December 1910, with a seasonal greeting.

93. Hanham Mills, still a place of relaxation. The 'Chequers Inn', on the right has been much enlarged, and you can walk along the tow-path from Keynsham to St. Annes. Card posted in June 1938.

94. Lawrence Hill. Lunch time in Berkeley Road! Workers from the Bristol Wagon and Carriage Works relax before the afternoon session. This is now the Lawrence Hill bus depot.

KINGSWOOD

95. Regent Street, Kingswood. All the shops on the left have been demolished and a shopping precinct erected. The white walled building facing right is now Barclays Bank, the building with pinnacled frontage dated 1892 an estate agent. The clock tower in the distance was erected by public subscription to commemorate Queen Victoria's Diamond Jubilee, 1897.

96. Picture House, Kingswood. A modern store now replaces the picture house and engineering works, though the facade either side of these buildings remains the same, with modern shops beneath. The building with protruding roof, in front of the van to the left of the picture, was the surgery of Dr. E.M. Grace, brother of the famous W.G. Viner and Co. of Bath.

31

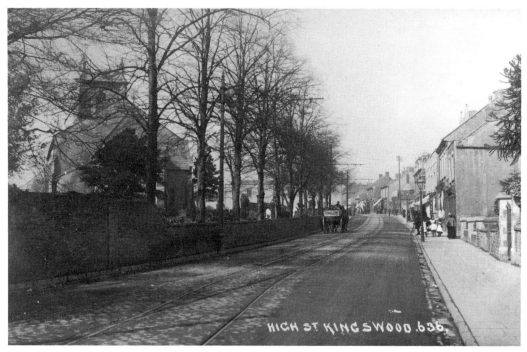

97. High Street, Kingswood. The wall, right foreground, is the end wall of the Linden Hotel. The trees on the left are a little larger now, obscuring Holy Trinity Church somewhat.

98. High Street, Kingswood, postally used 1912. Very little changed.

99. The Clock Tower, Kingswood. Still recognisable! Some household names on the shops on the right are Bearks Stores, Hodders the Chemists, Verrier, Tailor.

100. Tea Gardens, Coombe Dingle, postally used 1905. Mr. W. Lee was the proprietor of the tea gardens, which were very popular for outings. The donkey was used to haul water from the pump at the bottom of the Dingle. Published by Hardings (Bristol and Cardiff) in their 'Progress' series. Message reads : *"... just had a good bust-out at the table on the extreme right..."*.

101. Coombe Dingle, Nr. Bristol, postally used 1915. This cottage is just off Canford Lane, and is still lived in. Beautiful photographic postcard by Garratt.

102. The Old Mill, Coombe Dingle, c. 1900. This mill was worked by Mr. E. Ball and sons, who were flour millers. Harvey Barton publication posted in 1915.

WESTBURY-ON-TRYM

103. Fountain & High Street, Westbury-on-Trym, postally used 1914. The fountain has been removed to Canford Park, and shops now occupy the space where bus stands. The attractive sign-post has pointing fingers on each arm.

104. Tram Terminus and War Memorial, Westbury-on-Trym. The shop behind the tram is still owned by the same family, Mogford's. The memorial was set up in 1920, but the island has been reduced in size. A Garratt postcard.

HENBURY

105. Cottage at Henbury, Bristol. This is Blaise Hamlet, which was built in 1890 to house workers pensioned from the Blaise estate across the road. Nine cottages, each with a different design but blending as a whole, surround the sundial-pump. These cottages are still occupied, but the whole is now owned by the National Trust.

New Bridge
at Sea Mills.

106. New Bridge at Sea Mills, postally used 1927. This bridge was constructed in 1926 to carry the new road, the Portway, over the river Trym. To the left of the picture can be seen the Roman remains of the port Abona. Photo by Hepworth. Message reads : *"It looks wintry here but at present the trees are lovely"*.

Horseshoe Bend & Portway, Bristol
13752

107. Horseshoe Bend and Portway, Bristol, postally used 1928. This was the new road, opened in 1926, linking the port of Avonmouth with Bristol, the previous route being across the Downs and Westbury. A train travelling from Avonmouth to Bristol can just be seen on the right of the picture. Harvey Barton sepia postcard.

The most costly new road in the United Kingdom five miles in length, and varying in width from sixty five to one hundred feet, between Hotwells and Avonmouth cost £ 800,000.

Portway and Sea Walls, Bristol

108. Portway and Sea Walls, Bristol, postally used 1930. In 1926 this was the *"most costly new road in the United Kingdom"*, costing £800,000.

109. Shirehampton Road, Avonmouth, postally used 1921. This is still a dual carriageway, but crossed by the M.5 motorway. York Publishing Company, no. 1856.

110. Penpole Place, Shirehampton. Can still be recognised today, and is situated just off The Green, Shirehampton. A Viners production.

111. Kingsweston House, Nr. Shirehampton, postally used 1906. This elegant building was designed by Sir John Vanbrugh in 1710. It was owned by the Napier Miles family, and at the present time is used as a Police Training Centre. J.B. and S.C. 'Avondale' series.

112. Gloucester Street, Avonmouth, postally used 1916. This photograph was taken outside the Dock gates, and the area is virtually unchanged.

113. Avonmouth Docks, postally used 1903. This is the old dock at Avonmouth, which was started in 1868 and opened in 1877. Message from Frank reads : *"Still in the land of the living"*.

114. Avonmouth Docks. Royal Edward Dock, which was opened by Edward VII, accompanied by Queen Alexandra, on the 9th July, 1908. The old dock, pictured in no. 113, can be seen in the right foreground. Postcard issued to commemorate the Port of Bristol display at the British Empire Exhibition.

37

CLIFTON

Clifton Rocks Railway

115. Clifton Rocks Railway, postally used 1904. The railway was opened in 1893, and bought by the Bristol Tramway and Carriage Co. in 1912. It was closed in 1934, and linked this part of Hotwells with Sion Hill, Clifton. Message on card asks if Annie has an album yet, and how many postcards she has in her collection. Published by Stewart and Woolf.

The Clifton Rocks Railway. 291.

Zig-Zag Walk and Bridge, Hotwells, Clifton

116. Clifton Rocks Railway. The interior of 115. The cars were operated by water ballast, and the charge was ½d to come down and 1d to go up to Clifton. It was used by the B.B.C. to store equipment in safety during 1940.

117. Zig-Zag Walk and Bridge, Hotwells, Clifton, postally used 1911. This was used by many people (with plenty of energy!) to reach Sion Hill, from Hotwells. Valentine's postcard.

CLIFTON SUSPENSION BRIDGE IN CONSTRUCTION.

118. Clifton Suspension Bridge in construction, postally used 1904. Harvey Barton postcard.

Clifton Suspension Bridge nearing Completion

Bristol. Oct: 4th. 1904. N. Serre.

119. Clifton Suspension Bridge, nearing completion, postally used 1904. The bridge was begun in 1831 to a design of Isambard Kingdom Brunel, but because of lack of money, by 1853 only the towers had been built. The work was recommenced in 1862, using the chains from the old Hungerford Suspension Bridge. The official opening of the bridge was the 8th December, 1864. Card published by W. Brisley, Park Street, Bristol.

CLIFTON SUSPENSION BRIDGE. 73.

120. Clifton Suspension Bridge, c. 1915. P. & A. Campbell paddle steamer makes its way back to the Hotwells landing stage, and a couple take a leisurely stroll along the tow-path, by the bottom of Bridge Valley Road. The smoke on the left is from the Port and Pier Railway, which ran from Avonmouth. It opened in 1865, and was closed in 1922. Garratt photographic card.

Entrance to Zoological Gardens, Clifton.

121. Entrance to Zoological Gardens, Clifton. Bristol, Clifton & West of England Zoological Society set up in 1835 with 220 subscribers, among them Isambard Kingdom Brunel, W.D. Wills and H.O. Wills. The zoo was opened in July 11th, 1836.

The Mansion House Bristol.

122. The Mansion House, Bristol, postally used 1904. Alderman Thomas Proctor's house, given to the city in 1874, to be used as a Mansion House for the city's Lord Mayors.

PROMENADE & PROCTOR'S FOUNTAIN CLIFTON BRISTOL.

123. Promenade & Proctor's Fountain, Clifton, Bristol. Alderman Proctor's gift to the city, to commemorate the gift of Clifton Down to the city by the Merchant Venturers, 1861. Postally used 1912.

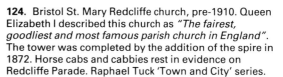

REDCLIFFE

124. Bristol St. Mary Redcliffe church, pre-1910. Queen Elizabeth I described this church as *"The fairest, goodliest and most famous parish church in England"*. The tower was completed by the addition of the spire in 1872. Horse cabs and cabbies rest in evidence on Redcliffe Parade. Raphael Tuck 'Town and City' series.

125. General Hospital, postally used 1907. The hospital was completed in 1862, and a wing was added over the warehouses in 1912; the dome has since been removed. The lock gate, seen in use, has since been sealed. Max Ettlinger's "Royal" series.

126. St. Mary Redcliffe church from the river. The elegant terrace on the right is still intact, but sailing ships are now absent. H.B. and Son, Ltd. publication.

127. St. Pauls Church, postally used 1905. This church was consecrated in 1831. In 1941 only the walls and tower survived an air raid, and these were incorporated in its rebuilding in 1950. The pathway to the gaol ferry was replaced by a bridge in 1935.

BEDMINSTER

128. St. Michael's, Victoria Park, Bedminster, postally used 1906. This church was built in 1886, and has remained unchanged. Published by C.S. and Co., Bristol.

129. Victoria Park, Bristol, postally used 1921. The houses of Totterdown can be seen on the sky-line, and Redcliffe Primary School can be seen on the left. Good array of fashions of the period. Published by M.J.R., no. 2814.

130. West Street, Bedminster. Although this photograph was taken in April 1939, it was felt it should be included. The tramway depot was hit by a bomb in 1941, and is now a used car lot. The E.S. and A. Robinson building, behind the tram, is still in use. The white house has disappeared, and is now a car park.

131. London Inn, Bedminster. There has been little change in the buildings, though a bank has been built on the right corner. The lady conductress on tram 99 dates this card as 1917-1919. Trams are coming from and going to Ashton, whilst the line on the left goes to Bedminster Down. A.G.S. and Co. "Chatterton" series, no. 299.

132. The Imperial Tobacco Co. Buildings, Bedminster. Solid but elegant building built 1901-7. The left corner now houses a bank. Posted in Bristol in July 1913.

133. Totterdown, postally used 1905. A very busy shopping area, since demolished for a ring-road that was never built. This was known locally as "The Bush", after the Bush Hotel, (not in picture). Postcard by Blyth, photographer, Bristol.

134. Wells Road, Bristol, postally used 1907. Looking in the opposite direction to 130. The Y.M.C.A. corner still stands supreme.

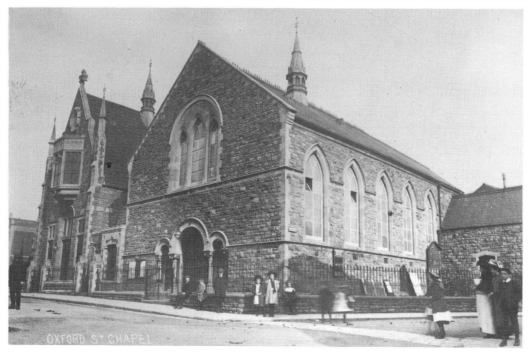

135. Oxford Street Chapel. This was a Methodist chapel built in 1874.

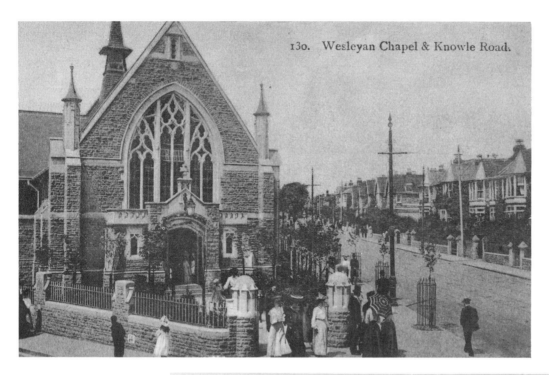

130. Wesleyan Chapel & Knowle Road.

136. Wesleyan Chapel and Knowle Road, postally used 1908. Completely unchanged, this chapel was also built in 1874. Newly planted saplings offer a great deal of shade now! J.B. and S.C. 'Avondale' series.

Wells Rd Knowle, Looking North.

137. Wells Road, looking North. The Talbot Inn on the right was a coaching inn when Knowle was part of Bedminster and outside the city. The houses on the right foreground are now shops. A Harvey Barton publication.

BROAD WALK, KNOWLE.

138. Broad Walk, c. 1935, published by Wilfred Loft, Wells Road, Knowle. The road has been widened, but the cricket ground is still used. The properties in the right foreground have been rebuilt as a shopping precinct. There is a concrete telephone box on the left, and a G.W.R. wagon unloading at Smith's the ironmongers. Card published by Wilfred Loft, 323 Wells Road, Knowle.

139. Bath Road, postally used 1911. Now a vast expanse of waste land. A road re-development scheme has just been completed. The turning on the right is Angers Road, and the Turnpike Inn, which was the old toll house, is in the distance far right. Grosvenor series, real photo no. 93P.

Bath Road, Bristol.

BRISLINGTON

140. Church hall, Brislington, published by L.T. Elson, Sandy Park Road, Brislington. At the junction of Brislington Hill, Water Lane, Talbot Lane and Bath Road. The hall was demolished and a new one built for use by the 'Executive Brethren'. Pump, horse trough and sign post are a sign of the times.

Church Hall, Brislington...

Brislington Village.

141. Brislington Village, postally used 1906. The 'King's Head', left corner, is still in use, as is the church. The building at the side of the tram is still habitable, but the forge next to the church is now a garage.

The Square, Brislington.

8776.

142. The Square, Brislington, c. 1900. Mr. West was the carpenter and undertaker in 1861, and the post office was opened in 1896. All this corner, to the Wesleyan Chapel, was demolished in 1970. The large house still stands, hidden behind trees. Notice the cobbled crossing, a common feature in Bristol.

143. The White Hart Hill, Brislington, c. 1910. The White Hart was a coaching inn on the Bristol-Bath road, and it was also a place for boxing, before the days of gloves! A milk float wends its way up the hill toward the farm on the right. Only the 'White Hart' survives, all else demolished for re-development. Postcard by Lilywhite, Sowerby Bridge.

THE WHITE HART HILL, BRISLINGTON. BLTN. 3

Copyright Lilywhite
Sowerby Bridge

Top of White Hart Hill.
Brislington.

144. The top of White Hart Hill, Brislington, postally used 1910. The gate is of Brislington Hill House, home of Mr. Cooke-Hurle, vice-chairman of Somerset County Council. It has since been demolished, and Glenarm Road now runs through here. A coal wagon belonging to Mr. Jonas of Keynsham wends its way home. Harvey Barton publication.

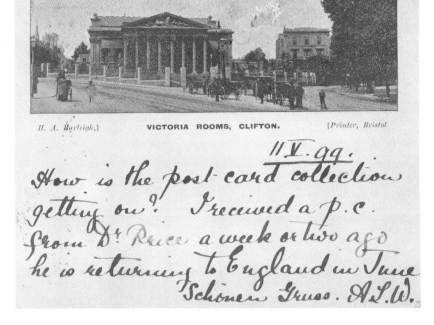

VICTORIA ROOMS, CLIFTON.

II V. 99.

145. Postally used 1899, court size 115mm x 89mm, approved by the Post Office 21st January, 1895, and in use until 1st November, 1899. Burleigh, the printers, are still in business today. Message reads : *"How is the postcard collection getting on? I received a P.C. from Dr. Price a week or two ago"*.

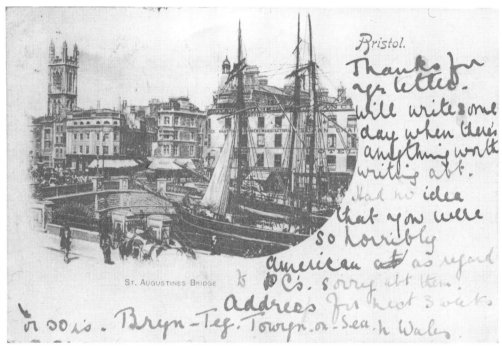

ST. AUGUSTINES BRIDGE

146. Postally used 1901, intermediate size, 130mm x 80mm. St. Augustine's Bridge.

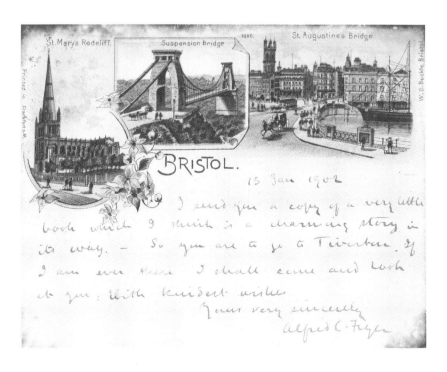

BRISTOL.

147. Postally used 1902, court size as 145. Printed in Frankfurt-am-Main. Published by W.D. Buckle, Bristol. It features three beautiful coloured vignettes.

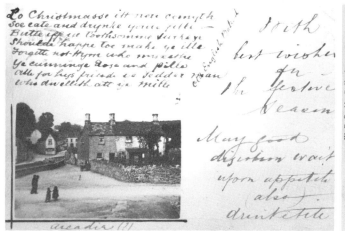

148. Postally used 1902, standard size, showing Dial House, Westbury-on-Trym.

149. Postally used 1903, published by W.D. Buckle, Redland, Bristol. Avon Gorge.

OLD PRINTS

150. Postally used 1901, posted in Belgium with Belgian stasmp, to a recipient in Belgium. Obviously a visitor impressed with his stay in Bristol!

VIEW OF BRISTOL CASTLE FROM THE BROAD WEIR, IN THE FIFTEENTH CENTURY.

151. View of Bristol Castle in the 15th century, built about 1050 by the Earl of Gloucester. Relics of the Castle Keep have been discovered, and are now deposited in Bristol Museum. A moat entirely encircled this fortress, and in the present day, its course is unaltered, but is arched over.

152. Temple Gate. Temple Gate stood near the junction with Pile Street, and was demolished in the early 19th century. Published by Fred Little.

153. Old Redcliffe Gate. This stood in Redcliffe Street, near the junction with Pile Street. Another Fred Little publication.

154. Fry's Chocolate, postally used 1913. A card showing the famous *Five Boys* chocolate advertisement. At this time, Fry's would have had their factory in the Union Street-Pithay area of Bristol, moving to Keynsham in the 1920's.

155. Puritan Girl. Advertising Puritan soap, manufactured by Christopher Thomas and Bros. Their building is now occupied by Gardiner Haskin, Broad Plain.

156. Window Cleaning par excellence! Public Window Cleaning and Carpet Beating Company, Stapleton Road, Bristol. It is thought the photograph was taken near Ashton Court Estate. Postally used 1907.

157. Photograph of tram 93 taken outside Staple Hill Depot, by E.J. Giddings, Mangotsfield. It was built by George F. Milnes & Co. Ltd., at Birkenhead, in 1896. Was in service on the Staple Hill to Zetland Road route. Rebuilt in Brislington depot before 1930, and broken up in November 1938.

158. Postally used 21st January, 1906. Thornycroft double-decker went into service on the Victoria Rooms-Suspension Bridge route on 17th January, 1906, replacing the horse-buses. Because they were higher than the horse-buses, there were complaints from the passengers on the top deck that the trees were getting in their way; consequently the buses were taken out of service for a time in 1909. Card published by Senior and Co., Cotham Hill, Bristol.

159. Motor bus at Hanham. Thornycroft single-decker, (with staircase for luggage to be put on the roof). Bodywork by United Electric Car Co. of Preston. One of the first batch to be used on service started on 5th February 1906, the route being Hanham-Longwell Green-Willsbridge-Bitton-Kelston.

Bristol Tramways Illuminated Car
December - 1924.

Bristol Tramways. Illuminated Car.
December. 1925.

Bristol Tramways Illuminated Tram.
December-1927.

160-161-162. Three trams decorated for the Lord Mayor's Christmas appeal fund, 1924-1925-1927, all taken at Brislington depot. These were the forerunners of the decorated buses which are used each Christmas for the Lord Mayor's appeal. No publishers identified on any of the cards.

G.W.R.—Bristol Station.

163. G.W.R. — Bristol Station. The Western end of Bristol Joint station, built in 1876, showing broad gauge track (7ft. ¼in.). This was changed to standard gauge (4ft. 8½in.) between 20-23 May, 1892. Published by Alphalsa, no. 1407.

JOINT STATION TEMPLE MEADS BRISTOL. 66.

164. Joint station, Temple Meads, Bristol, about 1900. Brunel's original station can be seen on the left of the card.

Interior of Temple Mead Station. Bristol. (1)

165. Interior of Temple Meads Station, showing the centre platform which was removed during renovations in the early 1930's. Published by Viner.

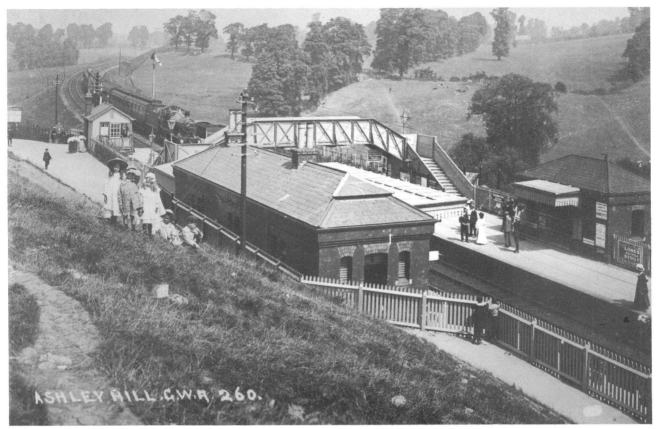

166. Ashley Hill, G.W.R. This was the line to South Wales and the North. The fields in the background are now covered by houses and Muller Road. A superbly-composed photographic postcard.

167. Interior of Clifton Down Station, showing decorations of July 9th, 1908. This was the Bristol-Avonmouth line, and the decorations were for the visit of King Edward VII to open the Royal Edward Dock at Avonmouth.

168. Sea Mills Station, postally used 1927. This is on the Bristol-Avonmouth line. Taken by a local photographer, Hepworth.

Colston Hall, Bristol.

Harvey Barton's Series.

169. Colston Hall, postally used 1905. The main hall was built on the site of an old Carmelite Priory in 1867, more being added in 1873. It was destroyed by fire in 1898, and rebuilt in 1900. A further fire in 1945 made it necessary to rebuild the interior as it is today. Published by Harvey Barton.

170. Bedminster Hippodrome, East Street, postally used 1911. Opened on 7th August, 1911 (postmark 13th September, 1911) as a Music Hall. Became a cinema and changed its name to the 'Stoll Picture House'. Damaged by the blitz in 1940, and now the site of Trident store.

171. Ashton Cinema, North Street. Opened in 1912, and changed its name to the 'Plaza'; after being a supermarket, is now a carpet shop. Published by A.G.S. and Co., Bristol.

172. Theatre Royal. Known locally as the "old theatre", the theatre itself is behind the frontage of three houses, which were built on the line of the city wall. This frontage was replaced in 1903, and again in 1972. This is the oldest Theatre in England, opening in 1766. A Fred Little photograph.

173. Princes Theatre, Park Row, Bristol. Known locally as the "new theatre", built in 1867, but sadly destroyed in the blitz of 1940.

174. Park Row, Bristol, showing the Coliseum Picture House (across the road from previous card). About 1912-1914, the building also included ice-rink and dance hall. In the first world war, part of the building was used by Parnalls to build aircraft. Later became a garage of Western Motors.

55

SCHOOLS

175. School of Industry for the Blind. Built in 1834, designed by Thomas Rickman, an E-shaped complex, the site is now occupied by the City Museum and Art Gallery, and University. Posted in December 1904.

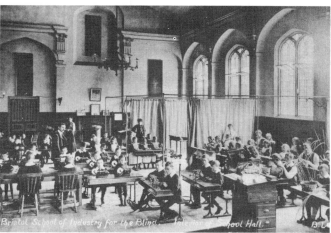

176 & 177. The interior of the Blind School.

177. Another postcard showing Blind School interior.

178. Ashley Down Orphan Houses, Bristol, postally used 1904. Built 1862, and founded by Rev. George Muller, it is now the Bristol Polytechnic. Published by William F. Mack, 52 Park Row, Bristol.

179. Girls from the orphanage off for a ramble. A Garratt photographic card.

180. St. Andrews Park. Muller's children walking in the park. Also by Garratt.

St. George's Higher Grade School,
from St. George's Park. 198.

181. St. George's Higher Grade School. Opened in 1894, founded by the local shopkeepers and local minister, the first Higher Grade School in the country. Postally used 1906. 'Ozograph' series, Bristol.

The Chemical Laboratory. St. George's Secondary School, Bristol

182. The Chemical Laboratory, St. George's School. This room is still the same today, except for the fact that the benches now face the blackboard. This card is one of an original packet of six which were sold for 4d! Published by W. Stackemann, Teddington, London.

Board Schools, Bayswater Avenue, Westbury Park 45

183. Board Schools, Bayswater Avenue, Westbury Park, c. 1895. Still in use, but not seen so clearly from the road, because of the growth of trees. Stevinson's "C" series, Bristol.

57

Clifton College

Nov 30·03

M.H.

184. Clifton College, postally used 1903. The big school and Headmaster's house were opened in 1862, and the chapel was completed in 1866. Additions were made up to the 1920's. Many famous people have passed through these hallowed portals.

Fairfield Secondary & Higher Grade School.

185. Fairfield Secondary and Higher Grade School, postally used 1905. Situated in Montpelier, and opened in 1898.

REDLAND HIGH SCHOOL, BRISTOL.

10010/52

COPYRIGHT.

186. Redland High School, postally used 1911. A girls' school situated near Redland Station. Burgess and Company's "Bee" series.

C. E. H. COLLARD, 94 REDCLIFT HILL, BRISTOL. MARCH 16TH 1905.

187. Collard's, Redcliffe Hill, postally used April 1905. The photograph was taken on 16th March, 1905. This firm of butchers has now moved to North Street, Bedminster. Used as an advertising card.

N. TAYLOR, (ESTABLISHED 1787.) Game and Poultry Dealer.

188. N. Taylor, Game and Poultry dealer. This firm was at 15, St. Nicholas Street. Notice the horse and carts to deliver orders, also the absence of the public health inspector! Published by Blyth.

MODES *Alexandra Drapery Co.* ROBES

Alexandra Drapery Co., Whiteladies Rd, Clifton.

Lest you forget where to come on Monday!!!

189. Alexandra Drapery Co. Whiteladies Road, postally used 1910. This store moved from here to Beacon House, before going out of business entirely. The message states *"Lest you forget where to come on Monday!"*. From one workmate to another? Published by the Irish Touring Picture Postcard Co., Charfield, Glos.

The Last Car to Clifton Downs

190. Scottish satirical artist Martin Anderson called himself 'Cynicus' and formed his own postcard publishing company in Tayport, Fife. This design is a good example of his popular cartoons with a transport theme, which were capable of being overprinted with any appropriate place-name. Cynicus, in fact, is credited with being the originator of this particular trick. This card was posted from Bristol on 25th February 1907 with the note : *"How would you like to be inside this car? I am just going to see your Auntie Marienne..."*.

Shall be waiting for You at

BRISTOL

I am picking up wonderfully at **SHIREHAMPTON.**

191. Published by Wildt and Kray of London. Series no. 2433. Another standard postcard with overprint. Postally used in May 1912.

192. Self-explanatory message! A card by E. Mack, King Henry's Road, Hampstead, London.

193. 'Greetings from Bristol' — 1905 postcard by unidentified publisher with city views inside each letter — another common postcard ploy.

LOCAL POSTCARD PUBLISHERS

Most of the publishers of Bristol postcards were small firms or sub-postmasters, catering for a very limited demand. Only a few, for example E. W. Savory, Charles Worcester, and Harvey Burton, published material of non-local interest. To research all the names on the following list would take a very long time, but the publishers noted here form the vast majority of those local concerns producing postcards in the early years of this century. The compilers would, of course be pleased to hear of any others, or indeed, to receive background information about any of those listed here. An * denotes that cards by a particular publisher feature in the book.

Art Printers Ltd.
J. Baker & Son, The Mall, Clifton
R. Barnett, North Street
* Harvey Barton & Son Ltd. (H.B.&S.)
J. A. Bickle, Whiteladies Gate
* Blyth
* W. Brisley, Park Street
Brown & Lloyd, Portland Place, Clifton
Burgess & Brown
* Burgess & Co., "Bee" series
Burleigh Ltd.
Castle Stationery Co.
Chappell & Co., Redcliffe Printing Works
M. L. Chubb, Shirehampton Post Office
E. Coe, St. Annes Post Office
A. E. Comer, Brislington
F. O. Coward, Bedminster
* "Dodson" series
H. Edbrooke, Clifton
L. T. Elston, Brislington & Bristol
Etches & Co.
* W. Garratt, 9 Station Road, Ashley Down
* E. J. Giddings, Mangotfield
A. E. Giddings, Abbots Leigh Post Office
Gray & Farr, 35 Abbotsford Road, Redland
Guillon & Son, Fishponds
Hardings, "Progress" series
J. A. Hamilton, Staple Hill
Haywards, 1 Corn Street & 49 High Street
* Hepworth, 66 Church Road, Horfield
W. Hepworth, 366 Gloucester Road
W. M. Hill, 19 Chelsea Park
Henry Hodder & Co. Ltd, Pioneer Cash Chemists
A. Hodgson, 64 Victoria Street
E. C. Hollister, Sandy Park Post Office
A. E. Hornsey, Bedminster Parade
* Fred Little (reproduction of Victorian photographs)
* Wilfrid Loft, 323 Wells Road, Knowle

S. Loxton, 7 St. Augustines Parade
* W. F. Mack, 52 Park Row
A. H. N. Middleton
Mitchell & Co., 30 Baldwin Street
* "Ozograph" series, 145 St. Michaels Hill
D. G. Parker, 4 Birchwood Road, St. Annes Park
Pincock Bros.
Plocknett, Kingswood
* M. J. R.
Rising, 156 Whiteladies Road, Clifton
S. E. Robinson, Shirehampton Post Office
* A. F. S.
* C. S. & Co.
E. W. Savory & Co.
Scholastic Trading Co.
* Senior & Co., Cotham Hill
* A. G. Shortman & Co., "Chatterton" series
F. C. Sincock, The Library, Westbury-on-Trym
A. E. Smith, 44 College Green
E. Snary, 26 Castle Street
W. A. W. Sprod, 101 Stokes Croft
E. C. Stevens, 12 Arley Hill
W. Stevenson, Bruton Place, Clifton
* Stevinson, "C" series
T. Stanley, East Street, Bedminster
F. W. Taylor, Clifton
S. J. Thomas, Boyces Avenue, Clifton
West Counties Agency, 14 Westfield Park, Redland
Wickhams Ltd.
Stanley Wood, Sea Mills Post Office
Charles Worcester & Co.
Wyman & Sons Ltd.
* York Publishing Co.
"York" series, 11 Lower Maudlin Street

Viner & Co., of Bath and Weston-super-Mare, also produced a number of fine postcards of Bristol.

BRISTOL : Area covered by the book

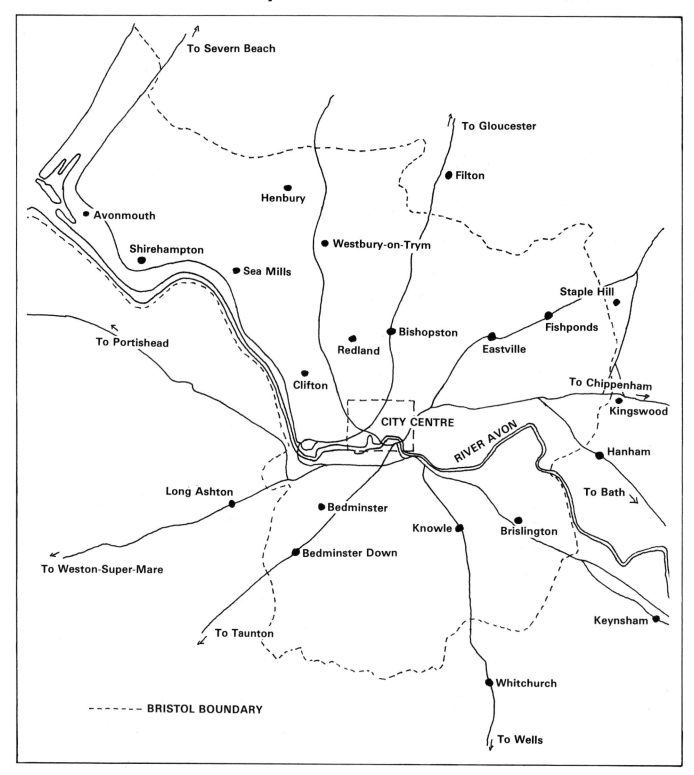

To Severn Beach

To Gloucester

Filton

Henbury

Avonmouth

Shirehampton

Westbury-on-Trym

Sea Mills

Staple Hill

Fishponds

To Portishead

Bishopston

Eastville

Redland

To Chippenham

Clifton

Kingswood

CITY CENTRE

RIVER AVON

Hanham

Long Ashton

To Bath

Bedminster

Knowle

Brislington

Bedminster Down

To Weston-Super-Mare

Keynsham

To Taunton

Whitchurch

- - - - - BRISTOL BOUNDARY

To Wells

NATIONAL PUBLISHERS

Most of the leading British Picture Postcard Publishers produced views of all the major cities, towns, and tourist resorts. Those who are represented by an illustration in this book are :

Alphalsa Publishing Co.
Boots Cash Chemists Ltd.
Cynicus Publishing Co. Ltd.
M. Ettlinger & Co. Ltd.
C. W. Faulkner & Co. Ltd.

F Frith & Co. Ltd.
Frederick Hartmann
Lilywhite Ltd.
W. H. Smith & Son
Stengel & Co.

Stewart & Woolf
Raphael Tuck & Sons Ltd.
Valentine & Sons Ltd.
John Walker & Co. Ltd.
Wildt & Kray

BRISTOL POSTCARD CLUB

The club's first meeting took place at the Swan Hotel in November 1981, with an attendance of forty. After a successful first year, an exhibition and fair was held in November 1982, mainly to publicise the club. An entry to the competition at the British International Postcard Exhibition (September 1983) secured first prize in the club section. Members also supply cards to the *Bristol Evening Post* for their "Changing face of Bristol" series, and cards have been exhibited in local libraries and building society offices.